PRIVATE LENDING IN AUSTRALIA

Power, Risk and the Rise of Non-Bank Capital

By Kalpi Prasad

Contents

INTRODUCTION

THE MARKET THAT WAS NEVER MEANT TO EXIST

Australia did not set out to build a private lending market.

It built something else entirely—a banking system designed for stability, predictability, and control. A system shaped by prudence, reinforced by regulation, and trusted by millions. For decades, that system worked as intended. It allocated capital efficiently, supported economic growth, and avoided the excesses that destabilised other global markets.

But stability has a cost.

It requires boundaries.

And those boundaries, while necessary, inevitably exclude.

Private lending emerged not because the system failed—but because it succeeded too well at defining what "acceptable risk" looked like. In doing so, it created a category of borrowers who did not meet the criteria, despite being capable, credible, and often profitable.

This is the paradox.

Australia's financial system is both strong and selective. It protects the majority, but it cannot accommodate every scenario. As the economy evolved—becoming more entrepreneurial, more property-driven, and more time-sensitive—the limitations of that selectivity became more visible.

Small businesses became more complex. Income became less linear. Property transactions accelerated. Opportunities became more fleeting.

The system, however, remained structured.

That tension—between real-world complexity and institutional rigidity—is where private lending was born.

At first, it was fragmented. Individual investors funding isolated transactions. Informal arrangements built on relationships rather than process. Deals done quietly, often out of necessity rather than strategy.

But markets do not remain fragmented for long when there is demand.

Over time, private lending began to organise itself. Capital pooled. Processes emerged. Intermediaries—particularly brokers—began to formalise access. Non-bank lenders scaled operations, drawing on securitisation and institutional funding to compete more directly with traditional banks.

What was once reactive became intentional.

And what was once marginal became material.

Today, private lending in Australia is no longer a shadow market. It is a recognised, structured, and increasingly sophisticated segment of the financial ecosystem. It funds developments, supports businesses, and provides liquidity in moments where timing is critical.

But growth brings complexity.

And complexity brings risk.

Private lending operates in a space where speed is valued, but mistakes are amplified. Where flexibility enables opportunity, but also creates potential for misuse. Where regulation is present, but not always prescriptive.

It is, in many ways, a market built on judgement.

And judgement, unlike policy, is not uniform.

This book is an attempt to make sense of that.

Not through theory alone, but through structure, behaviour, and experience. It examines how private lending evolved, why it continues to grow, and what must happen for it to remain sustainable.

Because the question is no longer whether private lending belongs in Australia's financial system.

It does.

The question is what role it will play in the future—and whether it will mature into a disciplined, trusted asset class, or repeat the cycles that have defined credit markets throughout history.

Chapter: The Cost of Learning the Hard Way

Before I built a lending business, I was on the other side of the table.

Like many entrepreneurs, I didn't start with perfect judgement. I started with ambition, impatience, and a willingness to take risks I didn't fully understand. Some of those risks worked. Many did not.

There were businesses that failed. Deals that didn't go to plan. Decisions made under pressure that I would approach very differently today.

And there was something else—something that shaped how I see this industry more than anything else.

I experienced what it felt like to be on the wrong side of private lending.

Not just rejected by banks—that's expected in business at times—but dealing with lenders and brokers who prioritised their position over the outcome. Terms that shifted. Costs that weren't clear. Pressure applied when there were limited options.

That experience stays with you.

Because when you're in that position, you realise something important:

The problem is not access to capital.

The problem is **how that capital is deployed**.

That was the turning point.

It changed how I viewed lending—not as a transaction, but as a responsibility.

When I eventually built Renown Lending, it wasn't to compete with banks. It wasn't even to compete with other private lenders.

It was to do one thing properly:

Provide capital in a way that I would have accepted when I needed it most.

That meant:

- Being clear on costs
- Being realistic on exit

- Being disciplined on risk
- And most importantly—being prepared to say no when a deal shouldn't proceed

Because sometimes the most ethical lending decision is not to lend at all.

This industry does not need more capital.

It needs better judgement.

And that is what I have tried to build.

CHAPTER 1

THE SYSTEM IS DESIGNED TO SAY NO

At its core, lending is an exercise in exclusion.

This is not a flaw. It is a function.

Every lender, regardless of size or structure, must decide who not to lend to. The criteria may vary, the processes may differ, but the outcome is the same: access to capital is selective.

In Australia, that selectivity is formalised through regulation.

The National Consumer Credit Protection framework imposes a clear obligation on lenders: do not provide credit that is unsuitable. This requirement, supported by ASIC guidance, forces lenders to interrogate borrower circumstances in detail—income, expenses, liabilities, and the capacity to repay.

It is a system designed to protect.

But protection, by definition, introduces friction.

Each layer of verification adds time. Each interpretation of risk narrows the pool of eligible borrowers. And over time, as regulatory expectations evolve, those interpretations tend to become more conservative.

This is particularly evident in the aftermath of scrutiny.

The Royal Commission did not introduce entirely new concepts into Australian lending. What it did was amplify accountability. It exposed failures, challenged assumptions, and reshaped internal risk cultures across financial institutions.

The result was not chaos.

It was caution.

Banks began to reassess not just their lending decisions, but their decision-making processes. Documentation standards increased. Expense verification became more granular. Policy exceptions became harder to justify.

The system tightened.

For the majority of borrowers, this change was manageable. For those with straightforward income, stable employment, and clean financial histories, the impact was limited.

But for a significant minority, the effect was immediate.

Self-employed individuals found their income scrutinised more heavily. Developers encountered stricter funding conditions. Business owners faced delays that undermined time-sensitive opportunities.

These borrowers were not necessarily high-risk.

They were non-standard.

And in a system optimised for standardisation, non-standard becomes a problem.

This is the critical distinction.

Banks do not reject borrowers because they are unwilling to lend.

They reject borrowers because they cannot lend within their frameworks.

Those frameworks are shaped by:

- Regulatory obligations
- Capital requirements
- Internal risk policies
- Operational scalability

Each of these factors reinforces consistency.

But consistency comes at the expense of flexibility.

Private lending removes that constraint.

It replaces policy with judgement.

Instead of asking whether a borrower fits within predefined criteria, it asks whether the transaction, as a whole, makes sense. It considers the asset, the timing, the exit, and the broader context.

This approach is inherently more adaptable.

It is also inherently more variable.

Because judgement depends on experience.

It depends on discipline.

And it depends on intent.

A skilled private lender can identify opportunity where others see risk. An inexperienced one can misprice that risk entirely.

This is why private lending is often misunderstood.

From the outside, it appears simple: higher rates, faster decisions, asset-backed security.

From the inside, it is far more nuanced.

It is a constant balancing act between opportunity and protection.

And it begins with a simple reality:

The traditional system is not designed to say yes to everyone.

Private lending exists because of that.

CHAPTER 2

FROM FRINGE TO FEATURE

Markets do not evolve in isolation.

They respond to pressure—economic, regulatory, and behavioural. The rise of non-bank and private lending in Australia was not the result of a single event, but the convergence of multiple forces, each reinforcing the other.

The first of these forces was funding innovation.

Historically, lending was constrained by access to deposits. Banks, with their established customer bases and regulatory backing, held a structural advantage. Non-bank lenders, lacking this base, were limited in their ability to scale.

Securitisation changed that.

By converting pools of loans into tradable securities, lenders could access capital markets directly. This not only expanded funding capacity but also introduced a new level of discipline. Investors demanded transparency, performance, and consistency.

The Reserve Bank of Australia has recognised securitisation as a key driver of competition, particularly in the mortgage market.

But funding alone does not create a market.

It enables one.

The second force was regulatory differentiation.

Banks operate under prudential supervision, requiring them to maintain capital buffers and manage liquidity in ways that prioritise systemic stability. These requirements are essential—but they are restrictive.

Non-bank lenders, operating outside this prudential framework, have greater flexibility in how they allocate capital. They are not bound by the same balance-sheet constraints, allowing them to pursue opportunities that banks may avoid.

This does not make them less responsible.

It makes them more specialised.

The third force—and arguably the most significant—was distribution.

The rise of the mortgage broker fundamentally altered the lending landscape. Brokers shifted power away from institutions and towards borrowers, providing access to a broader range of products and lenders.

In doing so, they normalised non-bank lending.

What was once an alternative became an option.

And once an option becomes viable, it becomes competitive.

By the mid-2020s, non-bank lenders had established themselves as credible participants in the market. They were no longer defined by their absence of deposits, but by their ability to deliver solutions.

Private lenders extended this capability further.

They operated beyond standardised products, focusing on bespoke transactions that required speed, flexibility, and judgement. They became the final layer in a multi-tiered lending ecosystem—one that could accommodate a wide range of borrower needs.

This evolution did not replace banks.

It complemented them.

And in doing so, it created a more resilient system—one that could adapt to complexity rather than reject it.

CHAPTER 3

REGULATION: THE INVISIBLE HAND

Regulation shapes markets in ways that are often invisible.

It does not dictate every decision, but it defines the boundaries within which decisions are made. In Australia, those boundaries are both clear and nuanced—creating a system that is robust, but not uniform.

At the centre is the National Consumer Credit Protection Act.

Its purpose is to ensure that lending is responsible, that borrowers are protected, and that credit is not extended where it would cause harm. ASIC's role in interpreting and enforcing this framework adds another layer of influence, guiding how lenders apply these principles in practice.

But regulation is not static.

It evolves.

It responds to misconduct, adapts to changing economic conditions, and reflects shifting community expectations. Over time, this evolution has led to a more conservative interpretation of risk—particularly in consumer lending.

This has consequences.

As standards tighten, the pool of eligible borrowers narrows. This is not a failure of regulation—it is an outcome of its design.

But it creates space.

Space for alternative approaches.

This is where private lending operates.

Often structured as business-purpose lending, it sits adjacent to the consumer framework. This allows for greater flexibility, but also requires greater responsibility.

Because flexibility, without discipline, leads to instability.

The most successful private lenders understand this.

They do not view regulation as a constraint to be avoided, but as a benchmark to be respected. They build internal frameworks that mirror the intent of regulation, even where the letter of the law does not require it.

This is how markets mature.

Not through enforcement alone, but through alignment.

Private lending in Australia is moving towards that alignment.

The question is whether it will get there before the next cycle tests it.

CHAPTER 4

THE ROYAL COMMISSION: THE MOMENT EVERYTHING CHANGED

The Royal Commission into Misconduct in the Banking, Superannuation and Financial Services Industry did not collapse Australia's financial system.

It recalibrated it.

Established in 2017, the inquiry was intended to expose misconduct across the financial services sector. What it revealed was not just isolated failures, but systemic issues—poor incentives, weak oversight, and a culture that, in some instances, prioritised growth over governance.

The immediate response was predictable.

Institutions moved to restore trust.

But the method of doing so reshaped lending behaviour far more than the findings themselves.

Banks did not simply adjust policy.

They redefined risk.

Before the Royal Commission, lending decisions often involved a balance between policy and discretion. Experienced credit officers could interpret scenarios, apply judgement, and approve deals that made commercial sense, even if they sat slightly outside standard parameters.

After the Royal Commission, that balance shifted.

Discretion narrowed.

Policy hardened.

And compliance functions gained prominence within decision-making frameworks.

This was not a superficial change.

It altered the internal psychology of lending institutions.

Every loan became a potential liability—not just financially, but reputationally. Documentation standards increased, verification processes intensified, and the tolerance for ambiguity declined sharply.

This created a measurable outcome:

Credit became harder to access for non-standard borrowers.

Not because they were less creditworthy—but because they were harder to assess within a tightened framework.

The Council of Financial Regulators acknowledged this risk, noting that institutions adjusting to heightened expectations could become overly conservative, potentially restricting the flow of credit.

In practical terms, this meant:

- Longer approval timeframes
- Higher decline rates for complex applications
- Increased reliance on automated or policy-driven assessments
- Reduced flexibility in structuring deals

For borrowers operating within straightforward parameters, the system remained functional.

For those outside it, the impact was significant.

And immediate.

Developers faced delays that jeopardised project timelines. Small business owners struggled to secure working capital. Investors found themselves unable to execute transactions within required timeframes.

The system had not failed.

It had become more precise.

But precision, when applied broadly, creates gaps.

Private lending expanded into those gaps.

Not opportunistically—but structurally.

Because while banks were recalibrating, private lenders were already operating within a different framework. They were accustomed to assessing complexity. They were structured to move quickly. And they were not bound by the same internal processes that slowed decision-making within major institutions.

This created a divergence.

Banks became more cautious.

Private lenders became more relevant.

But relevance brings scrutiny.

As private lending grew, it began to attract the same questions that had been asked of banks:

- Are borrowers being treated fairly?
- Are risks being properly disclosed?
- Are incentives aligned with outcomes?

These questions are not external.

They are internal.

They define whether the sector matures—or repeats the mistakes it was never designed to make.

The Royal Commission did not create private lending.

But it accelerated its evolution.

And in doing so, it set the stage for the next phase of the market—one defined not just by growth, but by expectation.

CHAPTER 5

CAPITAL AT SCALE: FROM PRIVATE MONEY TO INSTITUTIONAL FLOW

The earliest form of private lending is simple.

One investor. One borrower. One deal.

But simplicity does not scale.

As demand for alternative credit grew, the market required more than individual capital—it required systems, structures, and consistency. The transition from private money to institutional flow marks one of the most significant phases in the evolution of the Australian private lending market.

At the base of this transition sits **capital aggregation**.

Individual investors, while flexible, are limited in capacity. They can fund transactions, but not portfolios. To overcome this, private lenders began pooling capital—creating managed funds that could deploy across multiple loans.

This achieved several objectives simultaneously:

- Diversification of risk
- Standardisation of processes
- Predictability of returns

For investors, this transformed private lending from a transactional activity into an asset class.

For lenders, it created scalability.

But aggregation introduces a new requirement:

Governance.

Institutional capital does not tolerate opacity.

It demands:

- Reporting
- Risk frameworks

- Consistent underwriting standards
- Clear investment mandates

This is where the private lending market begins to resemble traditional finance.

Not in structure—but in discipline.

The next layer is **warehouse funding**.

Warehouse facilities act as revolving lines of credit, enabling lenders to originate loans at scale before refinancing or securitising them. Typically provided by institutional investors or larger financial entities, these facilities introduce a quasi-prudential overlay into the private lending model.

They impose constraints:

- Maximum exposure limits
- Portfolio diversification requirements
- Credit criteria thresholds
- Ongoing monitoring and reporting

In effect, warehouse providers become silent partners in risk management.

They do not originate deals—but they influence how those deals are structured.

This influence is critical.

Because it creates alignment between private lending practices and institutional expectations.

At the highest level sits **securitisation**.

While more commonly associated with larger non-bank lenders, its impact extends across the market. It establishes benchmarks for pricing, documentation, and performance. It also connects Australian private lending to global capital markets.

The Reserve Bank of Australia has consistently highlighted the importance of securitisation in supporting competition and providing alternative funding channels.

This connection to global capital introduces both opportunity and risk.

Opportunity, because it expands funding capacity.

Risk, because it introduces external pressures—market sentiment, liquidity conditions, and investor expectations.

Private lending, once local and relationship-driven, becomes influenced by global dynamics.

This is the point at which the market changes fundamentally.

It is no longer defined by access to capital.

It is defined by the ability to manage it.

And management requires discipline.

Because capital, particularly institutional capital, is not patient.

It expects performance.

It expects consistency.

And when those expectations are not met, it withdraws.

This is the cycle that defines all credit markets.

Expansion.

Optimisation.

Excess.

Correction.

Private lending in Australia is moving through this cycle.

The question is not whether it will reach the later stages.

It will.

The question is whether it will do so with the structures required to withstand them.

CHAPTER 6

RESPONSIBLE LENDING VS REALITY

Responsible lending is a principle.

Reality is a constraint.

The tension between the two defines much of the modern Australian credit market.

At its core, responsible lending seeks to ensure that borrowers are not placed into positions they cannot sustain. It requires lenders to assess capacity, verify information, and act in the borrower's best interests.

In theory, this creates a safer system.

In practice, it introduces complexity.

Because borrowers do not exist in static conditions.

Income fluctuates. Expenses change. Circumstances evolve.

Assessing a borrower's ability to repay over time is not a precise science—it is an informed judgement.

This is where interpretation becomes critical.

Different lenders interpret responsible lending obligations differently. Some adopt conservative positions, requiring extensive documentation and applying strict criteria. Others take a more pragmatic approach, balancing compliance with commercial judgement.

This divergence is amplified in private lending.

Because private lenders often operate in scenarios where:

- Income is irregular
- Timeframes are compressed
- Opportunities are transient

Applying standardised assessment models to these scenarios can be impractical.

But removing structure entirely is dangerous.

This creates a delicate balance.

Private lenders must navigate between:

- Compliance expectations
- Commercial realities
- Ethical considerations

The most effective lenders do not reject responsible lending principles.

They adapt them.

They focus on:

- Realistic exit strategies
- Conservative asset valuations
- Transparent communication with borrowers
- Alignment between risk and pricing

They recognise that sustainability is not achieved through documentation alone—but through structure.

This is where the concept of **"fit for purpose lending"** becomes relevant.

Not every loan needs to be structured as long-term, low-cost debt.

Some loans are inherently short-term.

Some carry higher risk.

The key is ensuring that:

- The borrower understands the structure
- The risks are clearly disclosed
- The outcome is achievable

This is responsible lending in practice.

Not rigid adherence to process—but informed, disciplined decision-making.

However, not all participants operate at this level.

As the market expands, variations in quality become more pronounced. Some lenders prioritise growth over governance. Others rely too heavily on asset values without adequately assessing exit risk.

This is where problems emerge.

Because responsible lending is not just about avoiding harm.

It is about maintaining integrity within the system.

The Australian private lending market is still defining its approach to this balance.

And how it resolves this tension will determine its long-term credibility.

CHAPTER 7

STRUCTURE IS EVERYTHING: HOW TOP LENDERS THINK

There is a misconception in private lending that decisions are made quickly because they are simple.

The opposite is true.

Decisions are made quickly because experienced lenders know exactly what matters—and what does not.

At the highest level, private lending is not about approving loans.

It is about **eliminating uncertainty**.

The best lenders do not ask, "Can this deal work?"

They ask, "How does this deal fail?"

And then they build structure around that answer.

The Three-Layer Thinking Model

Top-tier private lenders assess every deal across three interconnected layers:

1. Asset

This is the foundation.

Not just the existence of security, but its **quality, liquidity, and defensibility**.

Key considerations include:

- Location and market depth
- Comparable sales and valuation conservatism
- Liquidity under stressed conditions
- Legal position (first mortgage, second mortgage, caveat)

An asset is not judged on its best day.

It is judged on its worst.

Because that is when it matters.

2. Borrower

Contrary to popular belief, private lenders do assess borrowers—just differently.

The focus is not on standardised income metrics.

It is on:

- Track record
- Behaviour
- Intent
- Capacity to execute the exit

A borrower who has successfully navigated multiple transactions carries a different risk profile to one attempting their first.

Experience reduces uncertainty.

But it does not eliminate it.

3. Exit

This is where most deals succeed—or fail.

Every private loan is temporary.

It must end.

The exit defines the deal.

Common exits include:

- Refinance into a bank facility
- Sale of the secured asset
- Completion of a development
- Business cash flow stabilisation

The best lenders treat exit as the primary risk variable.

They ask:

- What must happen for this loan to be repaid?
- What could prevent that outcome?
- What is the fallback position?

If those questions cannot be answered clearly, the deal does not proceed.

Speed vs Precision

Speed is often marketed as the defining feature of private lending.

But speed without precision is reckless.

True speed comes from clarity.

When a lender understands the asset, the borrower, and the exit, decisions become faster—not because risk is ignored, but because it is understood.

This is why experienced lenders can provide indicative terms within hours.

They are not guessing.

They are recognising patterns.

The Discipline Gap

Not all lenders operate at this level.

As capital flows into the sector, new entrants emerge—some experienced, others opportunistic.

The difference between them is discipline.

Disciplined lenders:

- Decline more deals than they approve
- Price risk appropriately
- Maintain consistent frameworks

Undisciplined lenders:

- Chase volume
- Rely on optimistic assumptions
- Blur the line between structure and speculation

This gap becomes most visible during stress.

And it is where reputations are made—or lost.

What Discipline Looks Like in Practice

There is a difference between talking about disciplined lending and actually applying it.

At Renown Lending, that difference shows up in the deals we decline.

From the outside, private lending is often seen as opportunistic—high returns, quick decisions, asset-backed security. But the reality is less visible.

For every deal that proceeds, several do not.

Not because they cannot be structured.

But because they should not be.

Discipline, in practice, means asking uncomfortable questions early:

- Is the borrower relying on an unrealistic sale price?
- Is the refinance assumption based on outdated lending conditions?
- Is the timeline achievable given current market dynamics?

If the answer is uncertain, the deal is paused—or declined.

This approach does not maximise volume.

It protects outcomes.

The focus is not on writing more loans.

It is on writing the **right loans**.

That means:

- Conservative loan-to-value ratios
- Clear and credible exit strategies
- Transparent communication with brokers and borrowers
- Fast decisions—but only when the fundamentals are clear

Speed, in this context, is not a shortcut.

It is a by-product of clarity.

Over time, this approach compounds.

Brokers know what to expect. Borrowers understand the process. Investors gain confidence in consistency.

And consistency is what turns a lending business into a platform.

Because in private lending, reputation is not built on marketing.

It is built on outcomes.

CHAPTER 8

CASE STUDIES: HOW THE MARKET OPERATES IN REAL LIFE

Theory explains the market.

Transactions reveal it.

Case Study 1 — The ATO Pressure Scenario

A business owner accumulates a significant ATO liability.

Revenue is strong, but cash flow has been mismanaged. Penalties and interest are compounding. The ATO begins enforcement action.

A bank declines involvement.

Not because the business is unviable—but because the situation falls outside policy tolerance.

A private lender assesses differently.

They focus on:

- Current revenue trajectory
- Available security (typically property)
- A clear plan to extinguish the debt

A short-term facility is structured:

- Higher interest rate
- Interest-only or capitalised
- Secured by property

The loan resolves the immediate pressure, allowing the borrower to stabilise operations and later refinance.

The risk is not the debt.

It is the borrower's ability to recover.

Case Study 2 — The Development Timing Gap

A developer secures a site with strong fundamentals.

Planning is approved. Demand exists. But bank funding is delayed due to pre-sale requirements.

Time becomes the risk.

Holding costs increase. Momentum slows. Opportunity erodes.

A private lender provides:

- First mortgage funding
- Flexible drawdowns
- Interest capitalisation

The loan bridges the project to a stage where traditional finance becomes available.

The success of the deal depends on execution.

Delays can quickly erode margins.

Case Study 3 — The Transitional Asset

An investor acquires a property requiring refurbishment.

The asset is underperforming but has strong underlying value.

Banks decline due to condition and income profile.

A private lender structures:

- Short-term funding
- Moderate LVR
- Clear exit via refinance post-renovation

The loan enables repositioning of the asset.

The exit is dependent on improved valuation and market conditions.

What These Cases Reveal

Across all scenarios, the pattern is consistent:

Private lending is not about replacing long-term finance.

It is about **enabling transition**.

CHAPTER 9

BROKERS AND LENDERS: THE RELATIONSHIP THAT DRIVES THE MARKET

The private lending market does not operate on capital alone.

It operates on relationships.

At the centre of those relationships sits the broker.

The Broker-Client Relationship

To the borrower, the broker is more than a facilitator.

They are:

- Adviser
- Strategist
- Interpreter of credit

They translate complexity into options.

In private lending, this role becomes more critical.

Because the stakes are higher.

Short-term loans require precision.

Misalignment at the outset leads to failure at exit.

A strong broker ensures:

- The borrower understands the structure
- The risks are transparent
- The lender selected is appropriate

The Broker-Lender Relationship

This relationship is less visible—but more powerful.

Lenders rely on brokers for deal flow.

Brokers rely on lenders for execution.

Trust becomes the currency.

Over time, patterns emerge.

Brokers learn:

- Which lenders move quickly
- Which lenders honour terms
- Which lenders can handle complexity

Lenders learn:

- Which brokers present clean deals
- Which brokers understand risk
- Which brokers manage clients effectively

This creates alignment.

Or misalignment.

When It Works

When the relationship is strong:

- Deals are structured correctly
- Expectations are managed
- Outcomes are predictable

When it fails:

- Deals are rushed
- Risks are misunderstood
- Disputes emerge

The Hidden Reality

The best brokers do not send every deal to every lender.

They curate.

They match.

They protect both sides of the transaction.

Because in private lending, reputation compounds faster than volume.

The Power Dynamic

As brokers have grown in influence, they have shifted the balance of power.

They control access.

They shape perception.

They influence outcomes.

This makes them central to the evolution of the market.

Not just as intermediaries—but as gatekeepers.

At Renown Lending, the relationship with brokers is not transactional.

It is structured around alignment.

Brokers are not simply introducers of deals—they are the first line of assessment. They shape the quality of what reaches the lender. They manage expectations before a term sheet is ever issued.

That makes them critical.

But it also creates a responsibility on both sides.

For brokers, it means presenting deals with clarity:

- Accurate financial position
- Realistic timelines
- Full disclosure of risks

For lenders, it means responding with integrity:

- Clear feedback
- Consistent credit approach
- Execution when terms are agreed

Where this alignment exists, deals move efficiently.

Where it does not, friction emerges.

The strongest broker-lender relationships are built over time—not through volume, but through consistency.

And in a market like private lending, consistency is more valuable than speed.

CHAPTER 10

WHEN DEALS BREAK: THE REALITY OF CREDIT UNDER PRESSURE

Every lending market looks stable in growth.

It reveals itself in stress.

Private lending, by design, operates closer to the edge than traditional banking. It deals with compressed timeframes, complex borrowers, and transitional assets. When conditions are favourable, this creates opportunity.

When conditions shift, it exposes weakness.

The critical mistake many participants make is assuming that failure occurs at the point of entry.

It rarely does.

Most deals fail slowly.

A refinance that was expected in six months becomes nine. A sale campaign extends beyond initial expectations. Construction delays push timelines out, increasing holding costs and eroding contingency buffers.

At first, these changes appear manageable.

Then they compound.

Interest accrues. Liquidity tightens. Optionality narrows.

This is where the original structure is tested.

A well-structured deal anticipates delay. It incorporates buffers—lower loan-to-value ratios, conservative valuations, realistic timelines. It assumes that the exit may not occur exactly as planned.

A poorly structured deal assumes precision.

It relies on timing, pricing, and execution aligning perfectly.

When they do not, the outcome is predictable.

The lender moves to protect their position.

This may involve:

- Enforcing default interest provisions
- Extending the facility with revised terms
- Requiring additional security
- Initiating recovery action

In more severe cases, it escalates further:

- Appointment of receivers
- Forced asset sales
- Legal proceedings

These outcomes are not anomalies.

They are part of the credit cycle.

And they highlight a fundamental truth:

Private lending is not forgiving.

It is structured to move quickly when things go right—and equally quickly when they do not.

This is why discipline at the outset matters more than optimism.

Because once a deal enters distress, options are limited.

And time becomes the most expensive variable in the transaction.

CHAPTER 11

MISREPRESENTATION, DUE DILIGENCE AND THE LEGAL EDGE

Every lender relies on information.

The accuracy of that information determines the quality of the decision.

In private lending, where speed is a defining feature, the risk of misrepresentation is amplified.

Not always intentionally.

But often materially.

Financial statements may not reflect current trading conditions. Asset valuations may be optimistic. Liabilities may be understated or poorly disclosed.

Individually, these discrepancies appear manageable.

Collectively, they distort risk.

This is where **due diligence (DD)** becomes critical.

Contrary to perception, DD in private lending is not a formality.

It is the point at which the deal is validated—or dismantled.

It typically includes:

- Title and security verification
- Valuation review (formal or desktop)
- Financial analysis
- Legal structure assessment
- Compliance checks

When inconsistencies emerge, the lender faces a decision.

Proceed with revised terms.

Or withdraw entirely.

Withdrawal is often misunderstood.

From the borrower's perspective, it can appear abrupt or unjustified—particularly if expectations have been set earlier in the process.

From the lender's perspective, it is necessary.

Because once material discrepancies are identified, the original risk profile no longer applies.

This is where disputes arise.

Borrowers may challenge fees, arguing that funding did not proceed. Lenders may defend costs, citing time, resources, and reliance on provided information.

These disputes are not theoretical.

They are common.

And they sit at the intersection of:

- Contractual terms
- Disclosure obligations
- Commercial expectations

This is also where the legal framework becomes active.

Indicative term sheets are typically non-binding.

Formal loan documents are not.

Understanding the distinction is critical.

Because once legal documents are prepared, costs are incurred.

And once obligations are defined, enforcement becomes possible.

Private lending operates with fewer layers than traditional banking.

But when disputes arise, it becomes highly structured.

And highly enforceable.

CHAPTER 12

ETHICS: THE DEFINING LINE OF THE INDUSTRY

Markets are not defined by their best participants.

They are defined by their average.

As private lending in Australia has grown, it has attracted a broader range of participants—some experienced, some opportunistic.

This creates variation.

And variation creates risk.

The distinction between ethical and predatory lending is not always visible in pricing or structure.

It is visible in intent.

Ethical lenders ask:

- Does this loan solve a problem—or create one?
- Is the borrower capable of executing the exit?
- Are the risks clearly understood and disclosed?

Predatory lenders operate differently.

They rely on:

- Borrower distress
- Information asymmetry
- Over-leverage

They structure deals where the downside benefits the lender more than the borrower.

This is not sustainable.

Because while individual transactions may be profitable, the broader impact erodes trust.

And trust is the foundation of this market.

In the absence of heavy prescriptive regulation, private lending relies on **self-regulation through discipline**.

The strongest lenders:

- Decline deals that should not proceed
- Maintain conservative LVRs
- Prioritise long-term relationships over short-term gain

They understand that reputation compounds.

And that in a relationship-driven market, trust is more valuable than yield.

This is where the industry will ultimately be judged.

Not on its ability to grow.

But on its ability to govern itself.

CHAPTER 13

TECHNOLOGY, AI AND THE NEXT CREDIT EVOLUTION

The next transformation in private lending will not be driven by capital.

It will be driven by data.

Artificial intelligence is already reshaping how lenders assess risk. Traditional credit analysis relies on static information—tax returns, financial statements, historical performance.

AI introduces something different.

Dynamic insight.

Bank transaction data, real-time cash flow analysis, behavioural patterns—these inputs allow lenders to form a more accurate view of borrower capacity.

This has two immediate effects:

- Faster decision-making
- Improved fraud detection

Fraud, particularly in document manipulation and identity misrepresentation, has become increasingly sophisticated. AI tools allow lenders to identify inconsistencies at a level previously unavailable.

But technology is not a solution in itself.

It is an amplifier.

It improves good systems.

And exposes weak ones.

The lenders who integrate technology effectively will gain a competitive advantage—not just in speed, but in precision.

CHAPTER 14

GLOBAL CAPITAL AND AUSTRALIA'S POSITION

Australia occupies a unique position in global finance.

It is viewed as stable, transparent, and legally robust.

This makes it attractive to international investors.

Private credit, particularly property-backed lending, offers yields that are compelling relative to other developed markets.

As global capital flows into Australia, the private lending market will expand.

But expansion introduces complexity.

Foreign capital brings:

- Different risk appetites
- Different return expectations
- Increased scrutiny

This will push the market towards greater standardisation.

Not through regulation alone.

But through investor expectation.

The local, relationship-driven nature of private lending will begin to intersect with institutional discipline at scale.

CHAPTER 15

THE NEXT CYCLE

Every credit market moves in cycles.

Expansion.

Confidence.

Excess.

Correction.

Private lending in Australia is currently positioned between expansion and maturity.

Capital is available.

Demand is strong.

Participation is increasing.

But cycles are inevitable.

The next downturn—whether driven by property market shifts, economic contraction, or liquidity tightening—will test the market.

It will expose:

- Over-leveraged positions
- Weak underwriting
- Misaligned incentives

It will also reinforce:

- Disciplined lenders
- Strong structures
- Sustainable practices

This is where the industry will define itself.

Not in growth.

But in resilience.

CONCLUSION

A PERMANENT PART OF THE SYSTEM

Private lending is no longer an alternative.

It is an essential component of Australia's financial ecosystem.

It exists because the system requires it.

Because complexity requires flexibility.

Because timing requires speed.

Because opportunity does not wait for policy.

But with that role comes responsibility.

The future of private lending will not be determined by how quickly it grows.

It will be determined by how well it governs itself.

By the discipline of its lenders.

The integrity of its brokers.

And the outcomes it delivers for borrowers.

This is no longer a fringe market.

It is a system.

And like all systems, it will be judged by its ability to endure.

Made in the USA
Monee, IL
04 November 2026

67377458R00026